# the
# CAMEO

for my nana,
and all those whose eyes are a spectacle of love.

# contents

## I

## II

# III

Loring Street
Twin Signs
Byproducts
Maps
Archer's Aim
Fossil Fuel
Nelehm
Final Act
Sunken Sea

Baccalaureate
As if Solitary
Birdsong
Heart to Heart
Moon Phases
Perpetually
Penultimate
Porcelain Eyes
Magnetism and
Afterthoughts

Janelle Solviletti's *The Cameo* begins with an astonishing claim: "I wish to disunite the postulation that love and time are one and the same." And she proceeds, from there, to offer lyrical "proof" for this claim, through means wily "urban revolt" and "manmade revelation," relational "In sequence/ it seems you are immemorial," and sacred. Depicting with great pathos the damage of two souls intertwining, as well as the even bolder proposition that romantic disillusion itself is a mirage "I think I made you up" she invokes such masters as Whitman and Dickinson in her impassioned quest with virtuosic authority, creating "tiny vespers" in a world where "all is relative to light." Solviletti's metaphysical investigations into desire, disorder, and the natural world invoke a debut poet's declamations "I am nothing but my own end" as well as a finely-wrought argument for the powers of being to prevail against the temporal forces that oppose it. Step inside, and "luxuriate the moments" with an unforgettable new voice, who boldly proclaims "My lips are an index of sinners/ I'm not done speaking for."

---Virginia Konchan

...And by the way, everything in life is writable about if you have the outgoing guts to do it, and the imagination to improvise. The worst enemy of creativity is self-doubt. And you are so obsessed by your coming necessity to be independent, to face the great huge man-eating world, that you are paralyzed: your whole body and spirit revolt against having to commit yourself to a particular role, to a particular life which might not bring out the best you have in you. Living takes a very different set of responses and attitudes from this academic hedony...and you have to be able to make a real creative life for yourself, before you can expect anyone else to provide one ready-made for you. You big baby.

—Sylvia Plath, *The Journals of Sylvia Plath, Smith College 1950-1955*

# the
# CAMEO

Janelle Solviletti

# f o r w a r d

## I

Often, I catch myself wondering if a memory can be tangible. The mind is an index of moments in waiting stance, ready to be called forward. There is no order to this narrative—we can all reconstruct memories with ease among a crowded place or in the silence of the freeway on a car ride home. For me, it's always been the daylight which keeps secret the deprivation I feel to have a moment as unmarked as it once was. Perhaps it is true that those who act solely on the basis of deep emotion cannot make intelligible decisions. Those who think late into the night are bone-tired, jaded or just lonely. Or perhaps, those who are not afraid to outwardly display affection in all its intensity are the ones who encounter the truest displays of love—the lucky ones.

## II

This narrative is a cameo of love and its evolution, how it may carry on, pass by, arrive or reemerge. There is no real calculation, timestamp or shelf life. We all fall victim as slaves of the clock, unable to separate what is and isn't from its winding hands. I wish to disunite the postulation that love and time are one in the same, that one can influence the other with such grand order.

## III

I write to engrave these moments in permanence—because it's become effortless to hide behind the unknown and refrain from engaging with memories that stir emotional introspection. Time neither slows nor quickens the intensity of a memory—it can hold a space at the very core of us, immemorial and ignited from a subtle reminder or association, or maybe it is our brave souls that call it into existence with intention. Love is not made for those who are afraid of its resolution or after life, but for those who feel it without boundary, filled by its company.

# I

Some love was made for the lights,
some kiss your cheek and goodnight.
—The Lumineers, "Slow it Down"

God Owes Us

In the name of—I am sorry.
the floorboard led me
to your laughter and suddenly,
I am holding your arm which
frames the doorway and
the best of me is parked
in your back pocket
nearby, everyone's talking
yet no one says anything
perhaps, you should leave now

and then

we are leaving now, in record speed
for afternoon coffee
I shouldn't have played this song
it mumbles our truth and leaves
through the passenger side
as you open the door
I am dreaming
of what it's like in your eyes

I catch myself staring,
yours are down the river
looking for what's left—
press your forehead

on the car window,
watch what moves by
and listen to the last verse
can we leave now? I ask my mind.

Sinner

You were right. Our love
is dead. Right you are. It
was written with a pretext.
A first draft precaution
I never asked permission to read.
Did you know the author?
He wrote above sea level
while watching the people drown.
Farewell my love, there's no trace
in the margins of our storybook
for I've saved you—
my lips are an index of sinners
I'm not done speaking for,

Collectible Item

We are out of time, ageless, mad boy.
Unhinge from your urban revolt,
last week you were blazing through
love for beginners
God, luxuriate the moments—dear stranger,
you are empathetically far-off
in a bind with silent order
a blithe disregard to my speech
if I could guess, you are in hideaway
cleansing your soul on revolt
retreat on and on—visitor,
wear no worry
our edition was discontinued
is no more than a collectible
for display only:
please do not touch.

Brooklyn

Looking for rest
in the unsung
at a standstill
tired of sleeping on the floor
you told me
to skip rocks at the recollection
and watch as they sink
until there's nothing that
leaves me but you

it's all or nothing
or everything
at once
it's your side against mine
all but patience
I never believed
my own eyes,
think we woke up
in April

and suddenly,
the night is over
with velvet curtains
and we never looked back.

*1:04 a.m., train ride from Grand Central to Poughkeepsie, after The Lumineers concert in Brooklyn, NY.*

Luminal

O Captain, caught wind of your loveless voyage
            saw you there, dragging on
             above sea level
             landlocked
             tied up like a buoy
             with your chin up high
             weighty, watered down purpose

O Captain, saw you from afar
            in the night
            your mulish sway
            tilting to the north
            of my [dead sea]
            if only you knew
            this place was built for your visit

O Captain, what is the damage in letting you rest?
I see none.

Let it be known, your stillness does not calm
does not swallow murky waters

Shallow love dweller, what do you weight for?

Shall we continue in luminal measure
your signs will be lost at sea.

My River

This place is made
for the passerby
your leaving, I watched
as you ran downstream
and the lights flickered
the sky turned off
just long enough
if often we return
to a place that is unknown
at when
does it become
familiar?
this time
the wind steals
your last breath
it's clear now

we are on our own

you were once
before me
feet swaying
finding
the water's cadence
just long enough
for me to remember.

Ubiquitous

It is sincere when I say it was a genuine misinterpretation. He had pizza three times in one'day. He wore a corduroy jacket with dark blue jeans cuffed. I parked three spots to the right of his little green car. The moon was angled over the brickhouse bar in an unearthly way. Like an Ansel Adams photograph, everything black and white in between. The door which he opened promptly at my arrival swung open, accepting us. On the table, there were two Blue Moons he ordered to set the mood. I asked him when he last played guitar. He talked about a rock chord I didn't know. He said nothing and everything with his eyes, spilled beer on the table, cleaned it with his white table napkin, in that order. We could hear "Closing Time" coming from the back bar. It felt planned. There was some banter about his vocabulary and one vivid dream. He claimed that the second-to-last song was ubiquitous, like I could understand that he would be just that. As for everyone around us, they fooled around. Kept us in encasement. His ears and my mind. Tiny vespers and a hunch that I was full.

## Star-Crossed

Nowhere near the edge
of our own galaxies,
everything illuminated.
Eyes alight on skies away
wasting time, anyone's guess
until the stars show up empty handed
to salvage sundown—gone tomorrow
they put on their flashy show
leave us to unearth phenomena
fill the gaps in between
their shiny display and vanish.
It's no wonder we exist
on the underside of eternal
we're all an orbit away from collision.
Suspended matter, sightless
from all this interstellar travel
searching for salvation
beyond measure.

Paradoxical Wind

We were
sun dancing
on twenty-second street
puddle stomping
giddy as children
playing with shadows

we were
unknowing:
all is hushed at dawn

we were
night crawlers
lamp post dwellers
on your cul-de-sac

we were
unknowing:
all is relative to light

there is nothing
like a paradox
coming in loud,
fashionably late
when you/i
were we.

Yours Truly

Saffron sunday 'noon
we pose
at the river's edge
look in on its treachery—
your eyes were nothing
more than a poem's end
I read religiously
until we closed the sun
actually, no
we left
a place mark
on the house hushed
over the high grounds
I can't unsee the
autumn backdrop
mid-October
my cell
next to yours,
our place.

Fine Tuned

Adjust your orchestra—
it is clear that
you desire deliberation
exist on in mundane tones

you perform as planned
but your lips slip
nonessential words into mine
as you try
to remediate
this discourse in delicacy, beg me
to challenge this theory
travel around
my true intention

we are nebulous stars

I am no orchestrator
no astronomer
just an optimist.

Affection

You took a hard breath
and held me hostage

in your lungs
in the room

collapsing
sucking air

as if
necessary
to your existence

when you wanted me
in the dark
only then
did I feel your hands.

Route Nine Lover

It was poetic when we kissed // your lips clasp on to mine and linger // eyes reside in mine // just low enough // a slow burn // sea glass cutting my skin // I am nothing but an innocent bystander // unfolding in our aftermath // watching you strip with deep intention // what is the damage of two souls intertwining // followed by an unnatural order of parting //

I suffocate // pull at the ceiling // at altitudes above us // air that will let us remain // last breath of the night

An Oath to Arriving

Light a match
burn a moon daisy
and pause, unloose Angel
lock her up in your drawer
in silo with regret | noun | known

as keeper, circadian clock
you wake in cycles
trail along the bed trim
between dream state and less than truth
is you Angel, stoic
from this angle view
aglow in the day moon

wake me
with your way of words
so I may ask our shadows
to refuse parting

before a palace of
lasts could leave your lips,
my eyes arrive.

Time Lapse

You go by slowly and in sequence
it seems you are immemorial
a view without interruption
airborne on your escapade
craft these frames into a film scene
time has no purpose in our display
spanning from night to week to year in special effect
everything depends on your exposure
transitions in record speed

I tilt my lens as you go
create a compression
of this degree at which
you move from day to night
never to return
an analogue hour
a preassigned unit of value

you go by and by
reverse lapse.

## My Body

In summary
the night
was a transaction
body for pleasure
nothing in return
yet the origin of pain
came from midnights prior
when you told me
I was your outlet—
cite our beginning
when time marked us
and you told me
in the silence
on the drive home
that you
couldn't breathe.

By Day

Narrow my mind
move like anyone (everyone)
in ways you tell me
                    sway in expectation
                    tip-toe above afflictions;

I have you, have you not.

You left your laugh
 in the doorway
 soundless thief,
        unashamed of its slight

        confession—
        we all live in the crux
         of our past
        let the lull of my lips
            follow you home

By night, I recognize your face
        in fragments
        like a bad dream

Day-Dweller my Moon-Visitor;
        rest heavy on my pillow
            stare at the silence

　　　　　and you,
I was sure of nothing more than you.


Mid-morning, soon enough
　　　it comes to know me and is gone.

Cityscape

What shall we name this city, then
you ask from the overhang:
we live in two landscapes
without season // without dates
without any reason to believe
there is an end to sitting still
looking in on a skyscape at dusk
from upper atmospheres
with another, who pretends
there is no end to night
who is revolutionized by the sun
each time it comes back—
no use in getting swept up
in each freckled display
only to return to what's left
light upon light,
call it sun language, watch as it falls unclaimed
I am tempted with each gap of land and
shadowed high ground
exposing your dimensions
somewhere in between these odd degrees
without months to separate
breathing cool air from gasps of summer
is this city and its lure— keeps us coming back for more
never quite uncovering its coil in one trip,
nameless biography.

# II

The stars above, they shine so bright
as they light the darkness of the night
they glitter like diamonds
against the night's black velvet gown
and speak to many lovers
with an air of magic in its tone.
—Cam Toner

Repetition

The truth is
I am native
to my own intuition
darkness evokes
catastrophic subsidence
a second glance
is taxing on the eyes
the absence of light
feels predestined
the passenger seat
feels heavy with air
as if even my car
must commemorate
your existence
the truth is,
I collect moments
while thinking of you:
am nothing but my own end.

## Exit Wound

Dialect worth translation
you and I are a product
of experimental conversation
an exit wound
cut from the same sapling
an existential crisis
disguised as a midyear affair
we are arboreal animals
with a colossal downfall:
we exist as only, above it all.

Cosmo Gospels

The truth is everything passes
       we're all tired
       roaming around ourselves
       cosmic orbital trails
       far from perfect


You and I are the example
       the one where we fail
       yet come back
        triumph on and
       tank on trying times
       might we rest?


I don't like that word
       and contemporary book stores
       the place where
       people pull at the covers
       unearth injustice in seconds
       and walk away


Time is encapsulated
       it paces round
       my palm dance

blue geraniums
breathing my air
azure azure
what is left yet the sky?

Blow smoke at my submarine
before I sink
steal little insanities
from the craft
before you break the waters
get high off
my intellectual spirit
and ignite constellations.

On Self

Either silent or poetic
I create urgency before disaster
a living semicolon

measure the area from
my mind to eyes
calculate
the degree of difference
decimal the ten.sion
and create diversion

label me as emotional philosopher
nothing but my last nostalgia
pirouetting around the consequence
that my eyes hold knowledge
my mind will never know.

## Notre Dame

There is no compromise
in your color
sulking at the edge
of my bed frame
singing a rendition
of my word
before it's written
you fold in threes
blue from gold
divides
gold from green
trolls along the edge
of my collarbone
lingers on my sleeve
my thumbs
a perfect fit
for torn cuffs
sitting in pew with
your riven hood
and washed out emblem
while I make home
in your cathedral
recite ritual in your wear.

Broken Cassette

Your eyes lie from a long haul
pull like a dare and run home

I would truth to know
what they do with shadows
in the streets we were made of.

After Hours Confession

Your finest soliloquy
ends with another story hanging
on the other side of confession
is a secondary preservation

no one wants to be remembered
for what they left unsaid

and on this note
I disembark
among the masses
of people flowing
constantly, everywhere
at once
endlessly loud
how unforgiving
when there
is nothing left
to speculate.

Dear Watertown,

The letter burnt in the muffler
exhaust spills in your streets
black ink drips down Mass Ave.

the skyline traces my farewell
flying toward the rearview,
I must leave it there.

The freeway makes rights feel wrong,
left, you sigh
left me no choice
but to part ways from
the paint that grids your borders.

How lucky of I to travel
from Mount Auburn to Common
direction dividing
the ones who stay
from those who leave:

goodbye to you, Watertown.

Backpack Man

What brings you here?

What is gripped so tightly
'round your shoulders
 might you rest
 what has weighed you down?

Was it your eyes
that led your heart
to a place so familiar,
was it your heart
that led your eyes
in direction of the path?

Is it the way this place whispers
conversations you crave?

Backpack man,
what brings you here?
I wish you'd stay a while.

Matrix Man

Fleeing a culmination of yesterdays,
you emerge

with a curriculum that
head starts my sundown
disrupts my mind's order
with instruction.

Make a slight space
for all your subjects
select each
with sequential value
and digress—calling all royalty,
welcome to this treason.

We course over
a crossword of equations
display
compendium galleries
exhibit
chronicle warfare

citation: you and I
are nuclear DNA

a series of arrivals
composed disruptions
tainting tomorrow.

Archaic

I don't know how we got here—
your head on mine
mine on 0 0 : 0 0
one ear transfixed
in an archaic dialect
dancing on the rim
a familiar hush—
ja sam sam/ I am alone

            But at least I know
            by your undertones
            that there was no rehearsal.

Are we allowed to do this
I guess it is too early to decide—
jednog dana/ one day
you recite the dénouement
I could have predicted
you and I were at its end.
Your closing remarks leave
            no room for response
                    only repercussions
                            of a native foreign.
I'll have the same tomorrow,
until I am able to recite our conclusion:
I know how we got here.

Runner

I could trace the Charles River
with my eyes shut
feet dragging along its dirt path
every Sunday at sunup—

it's spring and the air is cool
people brush by in limbo
take no notice that
the sky is auto-tuned
the paint stripped bench
at the river's edge
has sunken in
or that the geese
disband the pedway —

but I run by and
watch the water
pull in and out
teasing the shoreline
persistent in its lure
the trees which shade us
are my canopy

my body is heavy
like a sandbag set
on the warm pavement

this is what it's like in oblivion
for miles and miles
the only constant
between us is the river.

Devil's Tower

Take a breath and escape me
grain by grain
press your ear up on God's land
to hear a distant anthology
scaling your surface.

When the hard rain falls
like an early morning moon
speak only the truth twice
and bury it
among the flowering dogwood.

This is speech without sound.

Somewhere high up on Devil's Tower
your sandstone and shale wear away
tonight, you were born resistant
Survivalist of Erosion
tomorrow, your igneous layer exposed
the kind that was once hot enough to melt

What is the damage of this windswept landscape
what alternative is there in isolation
a place where all things leave,
grain by grain.

Pseudo

I was unaware
a moment
in this time zone
was nonrefundable

that coming and going
is not a carbon copy
of staying
it's just showing up
in a place that
we sang or sung—

bring back my ear
it's pressed up
on your vinyl skin

rapid eye movements
lost behind a dream

who knew
there is vanity
in forgetting.

Cloudburst

Cryptic note in his coat pocket on November's eve, when we were anything but a tragedian daydream. His hand graced mine in passing. I'll marry that girl someday. He was wrong. There was a winter between us, a night at the *Casa Blanca*, a slow drive down Dudley Road. Crunched up language in the passenger side for three weeks. I didn't tell of my rides to and from New York. How I glorified his songs to match my rhyme. I made us before he cracked the code that people only gaze at the rain aloof at the windowsill. When it falls hard, cordial like it knows you— the people run.

Emotion

The words spill forward—this is an involuntary act. I am detailing a love that has ended without detail. Soon enough, I am a volatile substance on clinical trial, arriving at the critical part of experiment with knowledge of the evolution waiting on the other side of truth. But he tells me from across the table at *Teatro* that we live in a world where we are only well liked if we surface contentment and are discreet in our sorrow. I idolize this as an exit sign worth taking.

Preach on, the deceptive and nonsensical verdict, so that I may object willfully and unearth a constant.

Trigger Word:

natural selection
welcome to the sum of my senses
set off from your theory
you write with no intention
to be forgotten or dismembered
stirred up a world
of systematic survival
with no realm of anomaly.

had you known
I would not survive
in your natural idea of order,
would you still refuse me?

rare among
your origin of species
too alive for your liking
I am empty-handed
hostility fitter than hospitality
rationalizing the legacy you lead

a host of vile disorder
lives on in my skin,

I stumble to select
the right word

to tell you
of my instinct
that you may desire
what I desire:
disorder.

Acrophobic:

Extreme or irrational fear of heights.

Rooftop mourning
the radio rants
above the city
in range of the station
you play when we drive.

On the outskirts
waiting on wakening lights
it dawned
in deafening silence
that somewhere in
the noise is you.

# III

...Ah, who shall help us from over-spelling
That sweet, forgotten, forbidden lore!
E'en as we doubt in our heart once more,
With a rush of tears to our eyelids welling,
Love comes back to his vacant dwelling.
—Henry Dobson, "The Wanderer"

Loring Street

Hallmark on the hill
adjacent to your home
where we stood
teasing and taking
stillness from air
memory to memory
time bound
only to return
midnight moon-drop
under lit street,
two shadows
closer than appear,
eyes made for the dark.

Twin Signs

Nothing is as catastrophic as the minutes
before a May sundown
three years olden
the empty elementary lot
your eyes
spellbound in my passenger window
entering tomorrow
my eyes
stuck on that dark ampersand
it seems we should not repeat
the song, the stars, the abundance of road
from this range
the cost of living in an unbuilt house
is one in the same with finishing a sentence
from one hundred and fifty-seven Mondays ago
time moves opposite of where I dwell
minutes away from the point at which
we begin.

Byproducts

im not sure
if you were sandstone and i was mudrock
                          or we were both made up of the
same fine grains
but i know we settled in a place
over time
and we were still.

im not sure how
but your collection
of particles collided with mine
and we were sedimentary rock symmetrical to the sun
                              tip toeing across the
Hudson
before we dissolved.

unable to resist the coming and going of each wave
an envious fleet of pulls
aware that we were always easy to break
over time.

we were still
for what seemed like centuries
                          and im not sure when but
pressure was applied
and we broke

from the same force
that formed us once
and now i am calcite and you are silica
and we're expelled on distant shorelines.

Maps

Blame disruptive innovation and fine print.

*Let bygones be bygones.*

You are nothing
but a transport link
from here to there.

Blame your lack of detail
as a relative dimension
learned in fine measure.

Projection:
you and me
we're thumbprints
pressed against paper
and then some.

You are a sphere
with no scale,
a manmade revelation.

Archer's Aim

I sent an arrow
across the sky
with a spine
sculpted to learn

you

the shot is aimless
heard by no one
trapped in hanging clouds

chanting for dizzy heat
in your direction
simmers of daylight
left in Oglebay,
West Virginia

what if it could bring you back?

we could tell tales
on the same treetops
where the sun sets
at a familiar angle
knee-high in a grass village
your bow is already drawn
worthless until you catch mine.

Fossil Fuel

In confinement
we construct criticism
into syllables worth sounding
it's summer again
meridian moonlit messenger
try the door in the backyard
twice shake its handle
with your eyes closed,
thief of the night
we are alone
upon arrival; a revolution.
Tip your hat
don't you love me?
Or do your eyes pass by
limitations:
I fossilize
the idea.

Nelehm [noun] / tune triggering vortex / a buried memory unearthing / the sunken one you suppressed / you are my memoir dismembered at birth / string together our story in pieces / pass me a Blue Moon from the school parking lot three years over / enter euphoria / beer foam tastes like honey comb / relive it in deciles / car light on wet pavement / stereo verse and undertones / static on static / please let the song end / conclusions worth lamenting / I think I made you up.

Final Act

The speed at which our bodies pull
toward each other is trivial—
you say
nothing is certain
dependencies like these
are yet another's love story
that will never be told
you found an alternative remedy
to make my heart heavy
for your atmospheric pressure

I beg you—keep us constant
no matter if consistent

in whichever or whatever momentum we travel
whenever
wherever
        we fall
        has no authority
        over our fate

however,
        you say
        is the weight
        in which we suspend
                headfirst, steadfast.

## Sunken Sea

Some things refuse to sink.
Your hand passes
mine wasting time for yours
in the distant night
we spun around ourselves
too stubborn to entwine
and simple it was
revelation on elevation
out of sight
in the side drawer
of the hotel room
with the Bible
and bodies
curving the shadowed room
if I am not yours
than whose?
the moon commands us
down the highway
in unison
singing like sailors
of a maritime realm
until it was no longer
in the hands of time
but in the hands of time.

Baccalaureate

Tucked the letter
behind the Hail Mary
like a prayer—

while we clapped
for a sinner
full of grace
hush, hush—

somewhere
in the chorus
is your confession

from a corner pew
at the hour of our end.

As if Solitary

I lean in to observe
your unknown
striding the length
of your coastline

reserve me as inlet
to your still existence
leave evidence
of our weathering
for the next wanderer
scattered in green memorial
yet safe in your shadow

what's left to be found
collects in your corner grove
I gather my body
at the edge of yours
landlocked in lakes view

the kind that
triggers celebration
returns with
relentless pursuit
of what has yet to
light my eyes.

Birdsong

It      happened     between     the     blank
spaces
     of     an     overplayed     verse.

Back-drop     hum     of     mid-
October.

The     start of     your     coming and
     going.
It
     happened
        in a stagger
           of blue plaid shirts
              and words drowned in
                  beer foam.

Call     it     an almanac     for     shadow-dwellers

     an illusion of     constants thrust into sunlight,

so it was,

not     knowing     whether     to be
remembered     or     forgotten.

The     chorus gets          harder to     recall
                 with age,

half-silence,                           half-filling in
the words

 like
           headmaster,
headstand,
 headfirst,
Headfirst.
Like the time you dragged me to your kingdom, cooing,
               lips full of grace, illuminant pink,
               hands built with unteachable stock
as if they would stay.
In off-tune beats
 I am cast in suburbia.
Chiseling      away at              a cardboard
cut-out
version
      of you and I,
until your eyes honor
     a         new        lyric,

and I'll return from my plea with no ears, hating that song.

## Heart to Heart

Small talk is self-absorbed. A loud distraction knocking at my memory bank. My mind is hard at work and well attended, sweats in psychedelic phases. Hues of color coruscating at my orb replace your commentary. I take no part in storing your weekend plans, the weather or Wednesday's front cover news. My mind is electrified. Drowning in a masquerade of truth. Unveil me a promise and I'll store it away to dissemble. You can blame me for this daydream I reconstruct at your feet. It is hard to love this talent and its legacy, to separate a real visionary when you meet one. My mind seeks to be used as a weapon. If you witnessed my love, you'd be first to know he built an empire of mystery. He let it burn by the gates before confession. I collected the fallen heroes and named myself as keeper amour. Never to decipher the phases between the glory of the golden hour and its destruction.

Moon Phases

We had forgotten
from all your
half crescents
and
moon dust
waning and waxing
that you could be full,
cast over the August sky
tonight,
you remind us
in phases
distance is relative
you are more
than left over
                    debris
collision happens within a
                    moment

                    and then some,
whether you are near or far
distance is directional
and you are the keeper
        of all ways.

Perpetual

Awake again,
singing that composition—
the way I remember the night
snow falling ad nauseam
the verse leaving your lips leaving mine

what a melodic catastrophe
remastered on my car radio
elementary rhythm ringing on
in memory of our last drive
the epitome of indifference
the opposite of what remains

nothing is compatible
to hitting replay for miles and miles          I pray
for rain/for resolution/for rendition
of your half-lit eyes shading
my passenger seat

what shall I name this feeling?
what is this last verse
leaving my rearview
the irony of silence
is right before you begin again.

Penultimate

Peane ultimus / almost last
Next to the last wooden church pew
home to late arrivers, early leavers
one and the same.

Conversations on Sunday morning
with our Father and my Father
who reads the Bible
as if this tongue were
second to none,
the long pause

before Amen.
We call on our last burning sins
forget to call
the ones before the last
like the night I say that
you are my ultimate.

You say,
we were long gone
like Dutch Alcon Blue Butterflies
Tecopa Pupfish or Javan Tigers

I say,
really, we were second to gone.

You say,
I have not seen the last of you
each time I mistake as absolute
you say,
I overlook the words before the pause,

You say,
you do not wish
to be second to last
in my series of things;

the foldable road map
the cassette tape
the minutes before
we should have been praying
on Sunday morning

the long pause


before Amen.
You say,
we should have gone to church
like all the other Sunday mornings
your hand pressed in mine

as if it were the last hand on Earth
as if it weren't next to the last
in my series of things.

        You say,
        you were taken for granted.

Porcelain Eyes

carve constellations
luminaries of the night
crack dusk into fragments
and dispel an arresting display—
all of you yet none of you
what a view under the sky
breathing in the aftermath,
all your translucent undertones
before they were scaled down
traces cast back in the valley sun—
but this geography unfolds itself
it goes without saying,
I am out of range
searching for new land
with a road map
destination: static scene
circa arrival times
circa departures.

Magnetism and Afterthoughts

It's called Entanglement Theory. It's really out there, quantum physics and photons and the idea that two human beings make up one entity and so no matter the distance between their particles will act similarly and timely. I did not care about Entanglement Theory until we encountered each other on the cobblestone downtown.

Einstein called it 'spooky action at a distance'. Maybe it was a mere coincidence that we were striding the same street.

I am left only to wonder still of the parallel between human emotion and the workings of the universe.

Magnetism and Afterthoughts

It was dark and it seems like a fall night because the air is crisper, tangy, hangs longer than usual and the breeze keeps catching the side of my face as I walk along the pier and there is a doorway at its end which I knock at and the blue chipped handle turns as I turn around to walk home, or to a place I thought to be home, and I am back at the boardwalk, and the ocean is ringing my ears, and when I turn to cover them, you are sitting there, and you say we must go far away and so we get in your car and everything reverses, me on the passenger seat, watching you drive.

Magnetism and Afterthoughts

In a studio apartment everything feels colossal, what's left unsaid from last night is plastered on the walls behind the clock, trickles through the doorway and enters me, feels astronomical in my chest. I try to remember the feeling of you before it escapes me slowly, burns the roofs of my feet. I am a bad drunk poet.

\* \* \*

Yesterday I bought my first record. I play the song *When We Drive* slowly on repeat on the freeway. I think of the night we did, for hours. Were you ever real or just a masquerade of fleeting love, perhaps a fragment of the imagination, a dream worth reliving, and I'll think of your soul in those moments: forever ago.

Magnetism and Afterthoughts

Familiarity
at first, so very far
and before I can realize
she has arrived.

Dark nights weave in and out
while mine faster than the kin
with monotonous repetition
around the sacred space I'm in.

The palace of cerebral enrichment
takes opposition at breakneck speed
dreams severed into mince meat
mixed generously with lions feed.

Those we trust, the authentic beasts
succumb to mediocrity
and strand the mad to live old boys
who long to be set free.

*--Anonymous*

Magnetism and Afterthoughts

Do you ever feel like you can't describe an emotion inside you—like there isn't a word that exists—like maybe there isn't one because maybe no one else feels it? I think there is no word for the feeling I have when I think about us, not you and I as we are now, separate beings, but when we were firstly and lastly us. Maybe one day I will find a word to describe that feeling that suits time as it was, perfectly still, against as it is now.

Magnetism and Afterthoughts

This is fiction falling for fate and looking away
your shadow slipping into the sun and its glare
caught up in a summer glance secret
this is we meet again holding tongues
and what they say about us
how some things refuse to change
like my eyes fractured in August
and your remarks folding into mine
what brings us back to the start
two lovers on the brink of dying
inventing a life around themselves—
this is rebellion youth on repeat eyes on eyes
vengeance and postscript,
making love on the passenger side.

Magnetism and Afterthoughts

Left room in the line breaks
to relive you in fragments
in time, magnetism and afterthoughts:
meet me in the halfway
shifting eyes in narrow hallways
spilt beer on sweaters
songs in sync at midnight
enigma on enigma
secrets in the snow
in October skies
in concert halls
on the train ride
your stride next to mine
in passing in phone calls
in pure language spellbound
in the *see you soon*
stuck in-between
self-control and desire
we are alone again.

we are magnetars; made up
of what's left behind,
intensities above it all—
never to be seen by the naked eye
celestial bodies in hiding
separate from the façade
conditioned on time
and its weakness
bewildered by its attempt
to conclude a force above it all: you and I as we.

Janelle Solviletti is a twenty-five-year-old writer from the outskirts of Boston. She graduated from Marist College in Poughkeepsie, New York, with a Master's Degree in Marketing. *The Cameo* is her debut poetry book, which encapsulates the tensions between time and love and their competing entities. She believes that it is the visionary who can call a moment into existence without the help or hindrance of the hands of time. She hopes those who delve into her poetry will recollect moments and commemorate those relationships with others, the natural world, passions and past times; whatever it may be that was once taken for granted by time's natural order.

Janelle's previous work has appeared in *The Feathertale Review* and *The Somerville Times.*

Made in the USA
Middletown, DE
06 July 2022

68620102R00057